DID YOU KNOW?

This book, and other food allergy books, may not be
discoverable to parents looking for support,
unless it is recommended with reviews by customers!

If you are a parent, advocate or educator,
please consider leaving a review for this book, as well as other
food allergy awareness resources, that help keep our children safe!

Your support could help save a life.

SCAN TO REVIEW

Someone in our CLASS has FOOD ALLERGIES

By Food Allergy Mom and Food Allergy Advocate
Hailee Oman

This book is intended to
educate teachers and children ages 3-8.

We can also help keep our friend safe
by washing our hands after we eat!
Why? Just in case any of our food sticks to
our hands after we eat!

"What if our friend accidentally eats or touches a food that is not safe for them?"

We need to tell a teacher or a grown up FAST!
You can be a hero and save their life!

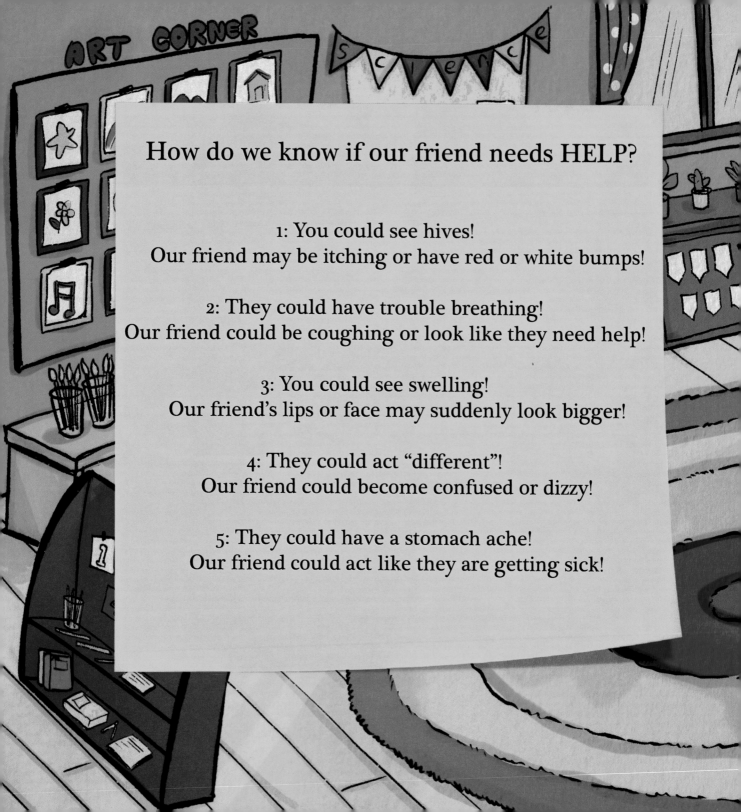

How do we know if our friend needs HELP?

1: You could see hives!
Our friend may be itching or have red or white bumps!

2: They could have trouble breathing!
Our friend could be coughing or look like they need help!

3: You could see swelling!
Our friend's lips or face may suddenly look bigger!

4: They could act "different"!
Our friend could become confused or dizzy!

5: They could have a stomach ache!
Our friend could act like they are getting sick!

What should we do if our friend has any of these signs?

TELL A GROWN UP!

That's why it is so important
that we know how to help them in case this happens!

If our friend is showing signs of sickness,
or if we KNOW they ate something unsafe,
they may need medicine, QUICK!

This medicine will help them so they don't get sicker!

We should NEVER tease or purposely
touch our friend with food they can't have!

You can get in BIG trouble,
and make our friend really, really sick!

Our friend is just like you and me!
They still love to paint, color, laugh, sing,
play games and more!

They just eat differently, and have to be more careful!

FOR EDUCATORS ONLY

PLEASE READ

It could save a life!

QUICK STATISTICS

32 Million Americans
are living with potentially life-threatening food allergies.

There was a 377% Increase in treatment of diagnosed anaphylactic reactions to food between 2007 and 2016.

Every 3 Minutes
a food allergy reaction sends someone to the emergency room.

1 in 3 children
with food allergies reports being bullied as a result.

Once a serious allergic reaction (anaphylaxis) starts, the drug epinephrine is the ONLY effective treatment

Approximately 20-25 percent of epinephrine administrations in schools involve individuals whose allergy was UNKNOWN at the time of the reaction.

Not treating anaphylaxis promptly with epinephrine increases the risk of a fatal reaction.

Most fatal food allergy reactions are triggered by food consumed outside the home.

There is no such thing as a MILD food allergy. A true food allergy has the potential to kill.

Researchers estimate that 32 million Americans have food allergies, including 5.6 million children under age 18. That's one in 13 children, or roughly two in every classroom.

Source: FoodAllergy.Org

DID YOU KNOW?

1. An **INTOLERANCE** makes one **SICK!**
   A **FOOD ALLERGY** has the potential to **KILL!**

2. **ONE DROP** is enough to cause anaphylaxis!
   The amount of the exposure does **NOT** determine the reaction severity!

3. Every single exposure can have a completely different **REACTION!**

4. Anaphylaxis can occur within seconds, minutes, hours and in rare events,
   DAYS after an exposure! Spotting signs and symptoms is key to preventing
   and treating anaphylaxis!

5. Delaying epinephrine is one of the **BIGGEST** factors in fatal anaphylactic
   cases! Don't be afraid to use it! It's better to be safe, than sorry!

6. **ALWAYS** administer epinephrine **FIRST!**
   CALL 911, and **THEN** call the parents! Do not delay!
   More than one dose may be needed before EMS arrives if any symptoms return!
   (Adminster second dose in opposite leg, if needed)

7. If you do not know or have your student's Emergency Action Plan, **GET ONE!**

8. **ALWAYS** check to make sure the student has their auto-injector with them, or
   know where the supplied EpiPen/Auvi-Q is for the classroom! **EVERY DAY!**

9. **NEVER** give a food-allergic student **ANY** food without checking with
   the parent(s) **FIRST!**

10. **ALWAYS** tell the parent if a suspected exposure may have occured!
    A topical **OR** ingested exposure can cause anaphylaxis!

TIPS for TEACHERS!

01

NEVER keep an auto-injector under lock and key! EVER!

02

Have ALL of your students wash their hands when they arrive for school AND when they return from lunch!

03

Create a "NO SHARING FOOD" rule for the classroom and lunchroom!

04

Instead of treats, ask parents to send non-edible prizes, to celebrate birthdays and holidays!

05

Encourage school administration to conduct a staff-wide auto-injector training each year!

06

The auto-injector goes where your student goes! This includes recess, lunchrooms, assemblies, or tutoring!

07

Your student may be afraid to tell you what they are experiencing! Frequently check in with them, to ensure they are feeling well!

08

Make sure anyone who supervises your student is TRAINED to administer an auto-injector AND knows the signs for anaphylaxis!

Substitutes included!

09

Never give your student a snack that has not been PRE-APPROVED or PROVIDED by a parent!

10

If you have a question about a snack or product, text a picture of the label to the parent, to confirm it's safe BEFORE use!

11

If your student is in need of epinephrine, DO NOT wait for a school nurse to administer!

12

Food allergens exist in every day items, not just food!

Example: Did you know Play-Doh contains WHEAT?

13

Ask the parents if you have ANY questions, big or small!

14

INCLUSION is just as important as SAFETY!

15

Teach your students to properly cover their coughs and sneezes! Some children can be airborne reactive!

16

Labels are always changing! It may have been safe before, but it may NOT be safe on the next purchase! Check the label EVERY time!

This is what is going through your student's mind when there IS food in the classroom.

This is what is going through your student's mind when there is NOT food in the classroom.

What is an Emergency Action Plan?

FARE — FOOD ALLERGY & ANAPHYLAXIS EMERGENCY CARE PLAN

Food Allergy Research & Education

Name: _____ D.O.B.: _____

Allergic to: _____

Weight: _____ lbs. Asthma: ☐ Yes (higher risk for a severe reaction) ☐ No

PLACE PICTURE HERE

NOTE: Do not depend on antihistamines or inhalers (bronchodilators) to treat a severe reaction. USE EPINEPHRINE.

Extremely reactive to the following allergens: _____

THEREFORE:

☐ If checked, give epinephrine immediately if the allergen was LIKELY eaten, for ANY symptoms.

☐ If checked, give epinephrine immediately if the allergen was DEFINITELY eaten, even if no symptoms are apparent.

FOR ANY OF THE FOLLOWING: SEVERE SYMPTOMS

LUNG
Shortness of breath, wheezing, repetitive cough

HEART
Pale or bluish skin, faintness, weak pulse, dizziness

THROAT
Tight or hoarse throat, trouble breathing or swallowing

MOUTH
Significant swelling of the tongue or lips

SKIN
Many hives over body, widespread redness

GUT
Repetitive vomiting, severe diarrhea

OTHER
Feeling something bad is about to happen, anxiety, confusion

OR A COMBINATION
of symptoms from different body areas.

1. **INJECT EPINEPHRINE IMMEDIATELY.**
2. **Call 911.** Tell emergency dispatcher the person is having anaphylaxis and may need epinephrine when emergency responders arrive.
- Consider giving additional medications following epinephrine:
  » Antihistamine
  » Inhaler (bronchodilator) if wheezing
- Lay the person flat, raise legs and keep warm. If breathing is difficult or they are vomiting, let them sit up or lie on their side.
- If symptoms do not improve, or symptoms return, more doses of epinephrine can be given about 5 minutes or more after the last dose.
- Alert emergency contacts.
- Transport patient to ER, even if symptoms resolve. Patient should remain in ER for at least 4 hours because symptoms may return.

MILD SYMPTOMS

NOSE
Itchy or runny nose, sneezing

MOUTH
Itchy mouth

SKIN
A few hives, mild itch

GUT
Mild nausea or discomfort

FOR MILD SYMPTOMS FROM MORE THAN ONE SYSTEM AREA, GIVE EPINEPHRINE.

FOR MILD SYMPTOMS FROM A SINGLE SYSTEM AREA, FOLLOW THE DIRECTIONS BELOW:

1. Antihistamines may be given, if ordered by a healthcare provider.
2. Stay with the person; alert emergency contacts.
3. Watch closely for changes. If symptoms worsen, give epinephrine.

MEDICATIONS/DOSES

Epinephrine Brand or Generic: _____

Epinephrine Dose: ☐ 0.1 mg IM ☐ 0.15 mg IM ☐ 0.3 mg IM

Antihistamine Brand or Generic: _____

Antihistamine Dose: _____

Other (e.g., inhaler-bronchodilator if wheezing): _____
_____

PATIENT OR PARENT/GUARDIAN AUTHORIZATION SIGNATURE _____ DATE _____ PHYSICIAN/HCP AUTHORIZATION SIGNATURE _____ DATE

FORM PROVIDED COURTESY OF FOOD ALLERGY RESEARCH & EDUCATION (FARE) (FOODALLERGY.ORG) 5/2020

REQUIRE one for your classroom!
Visit FoodAllergy.org to download a
FREE COPY or scan here

How do I use the auto-injectors?

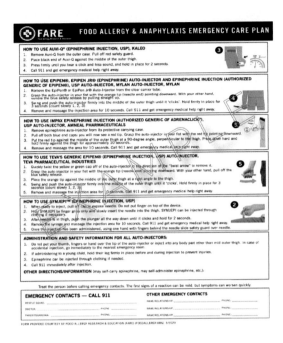

Scan here for instructions for
EpiPen

Scan here for instructions for
AUVI-Q

AUVI-Q® (epinephrine injection, USP) administers epinephrine in 3 steps.[13]

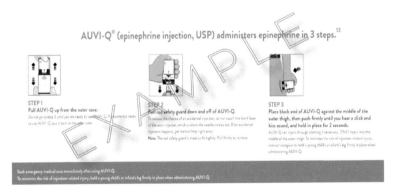

**Find more training and resources
at FoodAllergy.org or scan here**

Is your school following the
CDC National School Food Allergy Guidelines?

FIND OUT BY SCANNING HERE!

**Thank you
for being an advocate for your students!**

Food Allergy Safety Kids

REMEMBER! Can't Touch This...

ALLERGY ALERT
Certain foods may cause malfunction

SEVERE FOOD ALLERGIES DO NOT FEED ME

Keep Your NUTS To Yourself
I have FOOD ALLERGIES

*Food Allergy Shirts being added monthly!

Food Allergies for Beginners

Browse here, buy directly from Amazon!

Follow us on TikToc!

Entertaining Children's Books for Parents!

TikTok

Little Leaf Book Club

Scan QR code to follow account

d TikTok

Making Bedtime Reading FUN Again!

Funny books encourage READING!

COMING SOON

Includes full book readings from the club!

The FIRST Food Allergy Training Safety Book for Kids!

All subscribers will get a FREE ebook of every new book in the club!

FOOD ALLERGY SAFETY
BUTTONS!

Ideal for young children and supervisors still learning about FOOD ALLERGIES!

2 buttons for
ONLY $10
PLUS SHIPPING

INCLUDES 10 FREE
SAFETY DOT label STICKERS!

Exclusively at
www.foodallergiesforbeginners.com

NEW

Food Allergy Safety
LUGGAGE TAGS!

2 Tags
ONLY $19.99
Includes FREE shipping in the US

SAFETY FIRST

"Ideal for parents who travel with food for their child!
It gives them the best odds for their bag, that contains safe food, to avoid getting bumped or delayed!"

*This is not a certified TSA product.
This is a courtesy alert to notify airline personnel of the essential contents of your time-sensitive contents of your property.

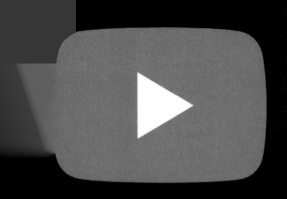

LEARN ON THE GO!

Watch the new "Is It Safe for Me?" A Food Allergy Safety Training Book, along with other family friendly books, on the GO!

ING SOON

Someone in Our Class has Food Allergies will soon be available on YouTube to send directly to your child's teacher!
Ensure your child's teacher understands the importance of the guidelines in place that will ultimately keep your child SAFE!

Brought to you by

Some ON THE GO titles are exclusive to subscribers!
Subscribe for free at www.foodallergiesforbeginners.com

Are you a food allergy advocate in the community or on social media?

Let's TEAM UP!

We do what we do, because we LOVE someone with food allergies, so let's do it TOGETHER!

Sponsor a page in this book and help make the world a SAFER place for those we LOVE!

Instantly Inquire Here

Awareness SAVES LIVES.

A message from the author!

My name is Hailee Oman! I am a mom, wife, publisher, and food allergy advocate!

My daughter was diagnosed with anaphylactic food allergies at 7 months old, discovered through breast milk. Now, 7 years later, I am still learning and advocating not only for her, but also for YOUR child!

This last year, my daughter was accidentally given cow's milk, instead of almond milk by a family member. Within seconds, she said her throat was burning, and seconds later, she lost her voice.

I administered an EpiPen in less than a minute of her initial complaint, which by then, she couldn't breathe. Thankfully, because of our quick actions, along with the help of medical staff that followed the event, we were able to save her life.

I genuinely believe if she had been around someone who was not prepared and trained, the outcome could have been dramatically different! This is an incredibly stressful, and traumatic realization!

This is just one of the reasons why I feel there is a critical need for this book in schools!

After 2 year, and interviewing over 50 teachers and food allergy parents, I had gathered extensive research to put this book together in a way I knew would be effective, and help implement food allergy safety and education in our schools!

During my research, I was alarmed to find that many teachers admitted they had minimal, if not any, auto-injector training- even though they had food-allergic students in the past or present! Additionally, an average of 90% of the teachers failed the "fact vs myth" quiz, spotting signs of anaphylaxis, and the proper response to prevent and treat it.

Many also admitted they were under the impression that the parents of food-allergic children were unnecessarily "overprotective". I believe, if they genuinely believe this, there could be intentional or unintentional leniencies with guidelines, and the risk of exposure and reaction dramatically increases!

We know this lack of awareness and education will eventually claim innocent young lives, if we do not come together to intervene.

I am so incredibly passionate about spreading awareness in schools, that I will soon be releasing a very powerful video, strictly for educating and training teachers and staff! Food allergy parents in the Food Allergies for Beginners Club will be able to share the video by email for FREE on www.foodallergiesforbeginners.com!
Please subscribe to be notified when it is released! You won't want to miss it!

Please take a moment to share this book, and other food allergy products, with other families looking for support!

I genuinely thank you for your purchase, and hope we can connect in the future,
as we build our food allergy community together!

Please join our Food Allergies for Beginners Facebook group, and let's connect!

Thank you again,
Hailee Oman

Website

Facebook Group

Will you help spread awareness TODAY?

IT ONLY TAKE A MOMENT,
AND YOU CAN MAKE A HUGE DIFFERENCE!

Please take a moment and rate or review this book,
and share it with other food allergy families on social media!

Your support could help save a life.

Made in the USA
Las Vegas, NV
12 June 2023